# *Endorsement*

Phyllis J. Bradley is someone that is ever willing to serve others in any capacity God leads her in ministry and in pastoral counseling. I have known her to be an astute woman of high caliber and I trust that you will be able to witness this through her writings. Journey with this author as she shares with us experiences from her heart and soul concerning the importance of obedience to His voice. "Behold, to obey is better than sacrifice and to hearken than the fat of rams" ( I Samuel 15:22 KJV). It is with great pleasure that I endorse these writings and am certain that every reader will be richly inspired and blessed by her words of wisdom.

Overseer Dr. Melveena D. Edwards
Doctor of Philosophy (PhD)

# COURAGE
# TO OBEY

PHYLLIS J. BRADLEY

# COURAGE TO OBEY

Printed in the United States of America

Publishing services by Selah Publishing Group, LLC, Bristol, Tennessee. The views expressed or implied in this work do not necessarily reflect those of Selah Publishing Group.

ISBN: 978-1-58930-311-9
Library of Congress Control Number: 2018913683

# *Dedication*

To my parents, James and Leola (who is now in God's presence), for giving tirelessly of themselves to provide a loving and stable home for me in an unstable world. To my sisters, Karen (who is also now in God's presence), Susan, and Leigh Ann, who in their own way played an important role in shaping the person I am today. To Eric, my love, my husband. My heart skips a beat when I think of how you love and protect me and call out the gifts that you see God has placed in me. You make me feel like a queen. Thank you for our precious children, Eric, Erin, Ericka, and Phillip (who is also now in God's presence). They have each truly been a blessing, not only to us but to the world. To Bishop Watkins, words could not express my gratitude for your kindness and consistency as a spiritual father. And to my Bebi and our granddaughter, Abigale Rose, who simply melt my heart. To all my friends and family, for "getting" me. And lastly, to Selah Publishing, for giving me a platform to share my understanding of how each person can spread the love of God in their own unique way.

# *Table of Contents*

# Foreword

As we know, there are so many different components that make up a book.

I am delighted to discuss this book. I have known the author for so many years, and I have seen her live out the thoughts of her writing. Obedience has always been Phyllis's strong point. That is why I can appreciate reading the words of a person whose life experiences have played out in real life and not just her writing as God awakened her ear to hear the guidance from Him and her personal experience.

Her hand held the pen of a ready writer, speaking of things concerning the King.

I am sure that you will be as inspired as I was reading this author's disclosure of her heart.

—Dr. Sherman Watkins

# *Introduction*

*Courage to Obey* is a book that will cause you to challenge the way you approach the concept of obeying. In a world that is driven by power and control, this book introduces another way to look at just how powerful the act of obedience can be when it comes from a place of pure love that only God can reveal.

*Chapter 1*

# The Dreaded
# "Four-Letter Word"

It's been my experience that whenever you mention the word *OBEY*, people tend to get a little squeamish. A lump begins to form in their throat, their heart starts racing, and any number of unwanted feelings flood in. What is it with this "four-letter word" that gets us so revved up? There is a certain negative connotation attached to it. It's such a small word, yet it packs a big punch! This word has been both feared and sought after, depending upon whoever happens to be using it at the time. This one little word has been considered so offensive that it's even been removed from some wedding vows. To include it could mean that one person is somehow "less than" or not as important as the other.

I've heard the word *obey* described as creating a demoralizing, dehumanizing power trip in conversation! Well, I not only can understand how a person could feel this way, but I can also agree—*if* the one belting out this COMMAND is the only one benefitting and if the motivation behind it is not right.

However, what if I were to suggest to you that this unpopular word, when acted upon with a better understanding of its broader meaning, could be quite empowering? Not only by the one requesting it—but also by the one who is meant to "obey."

In all fairness, let's take a closer look at this word *obey*. It comes from the Greek word *hupak-ouo*—*hupa* meaning "under" or "a place beneath," and *akouo* meaning "to hear and understand, to listen attentively." This definition gives us a little more insight. The Hebrew word *shama* means "to hear intelligently, to consider and consent with, a commitment to diligently discern or perceive or give ear to." In our modern era, *Webster's Dictionary defines* it this way: "1. to follow the commands, guidance or direction of; 2. to conform to or comply with, follow, conform and comply, require a decision to be made." All three definitions demonstrate that *obey* is an action word. These definitions don't sound degrading or intimidating to me (except maybe the "place beneath" part), but I'll address that later in an example concerning rank. These words actually sound empowering! It's as if the one being asked to obey has just as much to gain as the one or the entity he/she is obeying. Both parties stand to benefit when they're in agreement. In other words, there are decisions to be made after careful consideration.

Sometimes there is plenty of time to think about it, and other times obedience needs to happen right then. For example, in the military, when a commanding officer gives an order to fall back or retreat when there's a sign that the enemy's been spotted or is closing in, each soldier must decide if they are going to comply or take matters into his/her own hands. By complying, they stand a chance of saving not only their own lives, but also the lives of their fellow soldiers. On the other hand, by hesitating, either because they disagree with their superior or because they're simply cowering in defeat, they may end up jeopardizing the very men and women they're fighting with, ultimately causing lives to be lost. Some give orders, and others simply follow them. There are no two ways about it. The one who is "in charge" has the necessary training and information to make the call that the soldier is just not privy to. Without order, there would be chaos. So being under or beneath in rank or authority does indeed have its place.

We certainly can't all lead at the same time. I say that because I used to think that not everyone was a leader. I soon found out that we all lead in different ways. You don't have to be out front to lead. We have eyes on us all the time, even when we don't realize it. People observe our attitude and what we do, or like the old saying goes, actions speak louder than words.

This brings me to the whole point of why I was inspired to write about this particular subject. I wondered why this word got such a bad rap. Whenever it's mentioned, we usually think of a parent scolding a child, a pet cowering before its owner and their commands, or a slave being forced to serve their master. I want us to explore the positive side to this controversial topic, and at the very least, entertain the thought that we might just need to look at it a little differently. Perhaps we might even consider looking inside ourselves to see why we are so afraid to visit the mere thought of "obeying." Who me? Obey who or what? And why? We usually fear what we don't understand, and yet we won't even take the time to look into it any further.

What are we afraid of? Are we afraid of what it might cost us if, God forbid, we would have to do something we don't want to do? Perhaps we would be forced to admit that we could be wrong about some things. Now, there's a thought. This not only applies to words we don't fully understand, but also to different cultures, lifestyles, and worldviews. All I'm saying is that we should explore before we ignore. Life could be so much more enjoyable if we would just lighten up and stop taking issue with every little thing or allow ourselves to become so easily offended.

I finally came to the point that I realized that one of the reasons I was so afraid of the word *obey* was because of my own need to be in control. I was a very sensitive, timid child, seemingly afraid of everything. I was bullied, and I can even remember the day I felt stripped of my power. The feeling came over me so strong when I simply lost the will to fight. It was as if the life was sucked right out of me, and I remember feeling overwhelmed and defeated as if I was fighting a losing battle or giving up. My fight was gone. I surrendered it and eventually learned, as I matured, to take responsibility for my part in how I perceived things. It wasn't just that I was a victim, but I was such a serious child that I could relate to things that others paid little or no attention to. My perspective and temperament played a big part in how I grasped things. *Intuitive* is a good word for it. Some would say I was an "old soul." Being that way almost felt like a curse because I knew too much. I didn't want to be that way, but that's who I was.

Trying to fit in was a lot of pressure too. I put myself on a need-to-know basis in order to be able to not feel like I had to be in control all of the time and to keep others from controlling me. Let someone else who is "in charge" take charge and do what they do best—that became my motto, my way of coping. It became my place of comfort to simply let others lead. I went from one extreme to the other, which, by the way, melancholies tend to do. There is no middle ground with this temperament. No gray areas. However, when we refuse to allow others to do what we aren't as skilled in or that we do not have the authority to do, we cheapen our own experience in life.

I had to learn this valuable lesson the hard way. Holding on to a false sense of security can leave you feeling very vulnerable. Whenever we try to have too much control, that's when we feel the most "out of control." We end up with the opposite of our desired effect. Holding on too tightly only forces "it"—whatever it is—to slip right out of our hands, whether it's an outcome to a situation that we were certain would turn out another way, or a person we realize had a different plan than what we had in mind. I notice that I do quite well at the beginning of a trying time, but after a while my faith begins to fizzle out. I start to lose the courage to believe and practice what I know to be true and I tend to take my eyes off God and focus instead on my own limited understanding.

Thoughts begin to surface of how I will look to others when it appears that I am cowering under the pressure to conform to the old way of thinking. People seem to be frightened of the thought of obeying. "We're free," they say, and they're right, but they are free to do what? They are free to underestimate the power and the strength that it takes to find the courage to obey. There's a huge amount of freedom as well as a sense of peace that follows a genuine act of obedience.

*Chapter 2*

# Love... The Other "Four-Letter Word"

When I stopped avoiding the very thought of *obeying* and allowed myself to see the concept through the eyes of *love*, I discovered a whole new world! I understood that God's love was unconditional. I experienced a renewed sense of empowerment instead of a loss of power as I had originally feared would happen. Think of it: *Peaceful* and *empowered* don't seem to go together, but that's what is possible when we just let go of our tight grip on being the master of everything and begin to trust. Trust in what, in whom? Proverbs 3:5 admonishes us to "Trust in the LORD with all of our heart and lean not to our own understanding."

Now, wait just a minute! That first part I can do—but when you start asking me not to depend totally on my own understanding, that's where you lose me. No disrespect intended, but that's when it gets scary! Well, the Scriptures go on to tell us to acknowledge Him (God), the Holy Spirit, in *all* our ways and He will direct our path. I like the language of the *Message Bible* because it breaks it down and leaves no room for misunderstanding. It says: "Trust

God from the bottom of your heart; don't try to figure out everything on your own. Listen for God's voice in everything you do, everywhere you go; He's the one who will keep you on track." In other words, don't assume that you know it all. Trust the process without having to know all the details.

Once I understood it like that, I had to step away from having to know everything. How absurd to even think I could navigate my way through this cruel world in my own strength. When a pilot is flying from one destination to another, they have a flight plan that they must follow. I'm told that the bulk of the trip is navigating as smoothly as possible throughout all the weather and conditions that may arise in between. So, the art of it all is to navigate your way around and through all the hiccups, like storms, that are in the forecast, as well as the ones that pop up along the way.

When I was a flight attendant I learned some important lessons. Some kinds of turbulence can be picked up on radar and therefore give a warning of what's up ahead so that it may be avoided or handled with caution. Other times it comes out of nowhere, you can't see it, hear it, or brace for it. If I was up walking and turbulence hit, I had to hold on if it was considered light chop. If I was in the middle of doing my beverage service and it was considered moderate air, I would put the beverage cart away to avoid any accidents, such as hot coffee spilling on myself or the passengers. But if it was considered severe turbulence, I would take my seat immediately to avoid possible injury. If the captain or first offcer had any warning or time to call me, they would, but if not, I was to use my training—and my common sense—and secure myself.

People would ask me all the time if I ever got used to turbulence since I had several years of experience, and my answer remained the same. Though it is a familiar part of my job, I never get complacent. Each instance is treated with caution and the utmost respect for Mother Nature. I never let my guard down. I loved my job and the people I worked with, but I also loved my life! The whole airline industry is something to behold. There's no way it could work the way that it does (flaws and all) without each person doing his or her best to obey the rules and follow all guidelines and regulations.

The breakdown in communication can be a contributing factor in the downfall of any organization, community, or relationship. A sort of quiet strength, if you will, was unlocked within me as I began to realize that obedience based on love *is* love in its purest form! What is love, or better yet, *who* is love?

First John 4:7–10 tells us that God is love. His Son, Jesus, is love personified. Greater love has no man than this, that a man lay down his life for his friends. If you don't think so, just look at the sacrifice He made for mankind. Jesus said if that if we keep His commandments (obey Him), we will abide in His love, even as He has kept His Father's commandments and abides in His love. That is His commandment, that we love one another. Here, love is the motivator. He *became* obedient even to the death of the cross.

Notice the word, *became*. It means there was a process to get to the point of continual acts of obedience that led to the ultimate act, giving His life for ours. First Corinthians 13:4–7 gives us a perfect definition of what love looks like. When it comes from a sincere place and not a grievous one, it's no longer a chore, but it is done out of loyalty and confidence. It's accompanied by a type of excitement because the pressure is off of us to push past our conscience. It's hard to swim upstream.

When we choose to follow the wisdom of the Scriptures that says to do all things as unto the Lord, it changes our whole attitude. Imagine doing everything as if God was the only One whom you were trying to please. Without a personal relationship with God through the Holy Spirit's guidance in fellowship, and getting to know His nudges and promptings, in my opinion it is pointless. Our focus must not be on the person (human being) or the entity we are obeying, otherwise it *will* be a struggle and feel forced, and we will always be inclined to revisit our decision.

Whenever love is the determining factor or motivation for obedience, however, everyone stands to gain. I almost said *complete* obedience. Is there such a thing? Partial obedience is disobedience, and forced obedience is unwilling submission. How can you unwillingly submit? Isn't that an oxymoron? We submit for different reasons. Humbling ourselves at a time when we *know that* we could refuse and just stand our ground speaks volumes to the thought process behind it all. An inner discussion must take place before we're able to come to such a conclusion. In order to hear that still, small voice, we have to quiet our minds and tune in to our spirit.

One's intellect is involved and is not an absence of a person's right to choose, but there is an opportunity to profit from looking at the situation from another perspective. Let's face it, we only know what's in our own mind until we're introduced to a new way or are exposed to different information. How else are we to learn and grow? Life is full of lessons. This doesn't necessarily mean that we have to change what we know, or that it's even wrong; it simply opens up an internal discussion and dialogue, which offers more choices. In doing so, it will challenge us to think beyond our small scope of reasoning. How boring to be the end all, be all. It's dangerous to become stagnant in our thinking. It can stunt our growth and keep us immature and small-minded. What's left when we've *arrived*?

The last time I checked, we were all on a journey through this thing we call life. We should try to learn from one another instead of fighting every step of the way, only to end up feeling lonely in a world full of people. What sense does that make? This new-found information gives us a chance to ponder a different approach from the one we may be used to.

I'm not saying that we always have to change, but at least consider that there may be another way, or even a better way, to think about or to approach any given circumstance. At the very least, it makes for more interesting conversation when we have an open mind, which usually happens when we are secure in who we are. I find that we can only reach this level of love by first swallowing our pride and yielding to the One who knows everything: our Creator, our heavenly Father. Once again, it's your choice. One thing I love about God is that He won't force us to do anything against our will. He always leaves the final decision up to us. There are several examples in the Bible of people who had to choose; I'll share a few.

Abraham had to choose to obey the Word of the Lord and take his promised son, Isaac, up to the mountain to sacrifice him on the altar. His love for God was obviously stronger than the fear that would have caused him to disobey.

Ruth as well as Orpah had a difficult decision to make once Naomi laid out to them what their options were. She asked if they would be willing to stay and wait for her new sons to grow up, if she was even able to have any, so that they could marry.

Jesus asked the rich young ruler if he would sell all that he had and follow Him, but He left it up to him to make the decision. I think that we should remind ourselves of that while we're so busy forcing our beliefs upon others instead of presenting the gospel, the good news, to them and allowing people to decide for themselves.

When we act apart from love, we are operating in selfishness and we only want to have our way. It's called *manipulation*! I'm only sharing what I had to learn and am still learning. Once I backed off from a quiet form of that very thing and got over myself, I soon discovered that I had been acting out of fear. I wasn't really sure of what I believed—who wants to admit that?—and I became so rigid in my thinking until I refused to learn. What if I was wrong? I know, right, me? Ever met somebody who sticks to their guns *no matter what*? Chances are they are scared to death—or a narcissist, or both. Maybe they're just being a jerk, but again it's their choice. Here's something to think about: What if we all started seeing people through the eyes of love? Through God's eyes. That may sound mystical to some, or even cliché, but I'm a witness that it works. I mean a godly love (*agape*), because we are incapable of loving to that degree. I don't think it's humanly possible. It would force us to have to look right back at ourselves, and there's more truth in that reflection than we are willing to *face*—no pun intended.

It takes a certain amount of courage to stop running from that inner voice that keeps trying to get our attention, which can get stuffed down just like that rushed meal that causes indigestion. Most of us suffer from spiritual indigestion when we rush through prayer and devotions. Is it even possible to hurry through meditation? "I just finished my 'hurried meditation'." We will miss out on some lessons that can only be learned through patience and experience.

Love covers a multitude of sin. Every single, solitary sin *is not spelled out in the scriptures.* To the one who knows to do good and doesn't do it, to him it is sin (missing the mark). When we humble ourselves, it's a clear sign that we're getting closer to gaining the kind of truth that can set us free. This whole "humble" thing is not for the faint of heart—a term that is used to describe one who lacks courage. One definition sounded just like it was referring to me, people who like only safe and familiar things. Ouch! As I started maturing in my journey and accepting the "peeling back the layers" process, it was difficult at times for me to face. I was so grateful that He didn't show me everything all at once. The person I always thought I was didn't come close to who the Holy Spirit revealed to me.

I do appreciate the honesty, even though it was a hard pill to swallow.

*Chapter 3*

# Humble Yourself

*H*umility is another word that doesn't seem to be synonymous with power, but there is a connection—a quiet, subtle connection. We must love ourselves and respect others in order to truly humble ourselves. Only those with a keen sense of wisdom or discernment will be able to tell. It's much less painful to humble yourself than to have God do it for you. Pride goes before destruction. *Submission* is one of those dreaded words, as well. It means yielding to something or someone in authority or power.

Yielding is a cautionary move to avoid a negative outcome. In other words, we choose to obey, but we can be forced to submit. If it is against our will, it ends up being nothing more than legal compliance. Have you ever seen a strong-willed child being forced to do something he or she clearly doesn't want to do? I can assure you it isn't a pretty sight. There's going to be some rolling of the eyes, words mumbled, stiffened bodies, and that's the nice version. I remember when our kids used to say "Whatever!" to us. Nowadays the young people say, "Fine!" Adults do it too; we use "choice" words to voice our resistance. It really means, "Okay then, I'll do it, but against my will!"

Back in 2011, I had been experiencing a lot of stress outside of the normal everyday triggers, and I was not feeling my best. It was to the point that I could feel something was different this time, but I kept trudging on. I don't know what it is with us females that we tend to think we're superwoman, invincible, energizer bunnies! It's called pride. Anyway, being in denial is what it was for me. One morning while sitting on the side of the bed attempting to get up to prepare for a four-day trip for work, I sat there for longer than usual. I just couldn't seem to pull myself together. I heard my husband, my lover, my friend say to me in the most serious and loving voice, "Babe, I know you don't like to miss work, but I don't think you should go today. I'm taking you to the emergency room, you don't look good!"

Now, he had to put it to me like that because he knows the "real" me—the me that not very many people have had the pleasure of seeing. I can be pretty stubborn, and I don't like to be told what to do, but this day was different. I'd finally found the "courage to obey." How many of us realize that it takes courage to obey? It can be a daunting thing to relinquish control. I have been a giver all my life, a *caretaker* is a nice term for it, but had a hard time receiving. I believe I had so much fear in the past because of the bullying when I was young, and I vowed I would never let anybody tell me what to do again. Being bullied takes away a person's power and sends them into a perpetual state of feeling out of control and helpless. It felt like no one was there to stand up for me.

I guess I didn't understand that back then, because whatever courage I had soon melted away and turned into fear. I didn't realize it until that day when Eric spoke to me from a place of pure love that it was okay to choose to let him help me and allow myself to benefit from letting him make a crucial decision that I was not able to make at the time. He got me to the hospital just in time. I was having a mild stroke, known as a TIA. As several nurses and doctors rushed to my side and whisked me off to take my vitals, I felt like I was in a fog. It was a strange feeling for others to be tending to me. The look on Eric's face was one I don't recall having ever seen on him before, either. It was one of overwhelming concern, fear, and helplessness. I could sense that he deeply wanted to help me and protect me, as he'd always done in the past, yet he was unable to this time. I knew he had done all he could do.

I began to call on my God, my Lord and Savior, Jesus Christ, the only One who could help in this time of need. I'm so glad that I took the time to spend in prayer and listening for His voice to get to know Him in a personal way and to know His love for me.

After this life-changing event, I spent the next eight months getting to know my heavenly Father in a greater way, reading my Bible even more and praying often. Not just on my knees but throughout the day, I talked to Him just like I talked to any other person. I turned off the television, quieting myself and my mind like I used to do years ago, before I got married and had children. I was meditating and being still in silence waiting to hear His still, small voice. I remember asking for courage to face my fears. I had *no* idea how He would answer that request. Isn't that funny? I even thought I could control the way that God would do it. Am I the only one who has ever tried to control God?

*Chapter 4*

# The Choices We Make

*C*ourage as defined by *Merriam-Webster* is "mental or moral strength to venture, persevere, and withstand danger, fear, or difficulty." I've heard it defined as the absence of fear or even pushing past the fear. I prefer the latter definition, because at times I have had to muster up courage even while I was feeling fearful: Fear of the circumstances surrounding the decision I was wrestling to make. Fear of the unknown. Fear of the possible consequences or repercussions I might have to suffer. It's also been said that courage is feeling the fear and moving forward anyway.

Whichever way you define it, courage is very necessary in the world in which we live. If we are going to live our best lives, reach our goals, and impact others in ways we can hardly even imagined, it is going to require us to step outside of the things that are holding us back. To be able to trust, we must be willing not to have all the answers and be fine with that. What if we chose to face our fear and forge on to become a positive force and influence? Not only to those around us but to ourselves, as well?

We hear it said all the time: It only takes one person to change things for the better. The best way for this to happen is to be confident in who we are and know that we are enough, because we are fearfully and wonderfully made. When we are challenged to face what we know to be true and we are willing to walk in that truth, we open up the door to an endless number of opportunities to learn.

There are also several examples we can see in the Bible of those who chose to disobey and who therefore suffered a great deal. Adam and Eve are often picked on for their role in the Fall of mankind. It's all their fault, we often say. If they hadn't made the wrong choice, then we wouldn't have to suffer today. Maybe we should ask ourselves what we would have done in the same situation. There were huge consequences for not having the courage to obey the God who had created them, but because of the fear that it could be possible that they didn't know everything there was to know, that perhaps in some way, they had been given a raw deal and were being cheated by God, they made the wrong decision anyway.

I'll admit that I have felt that way before, as if God just doesn't want me to have any fun or enjoy myself, only to find out later that He knew more than I did—and that if I'd had my way, it would have been a disaster! Remember the Tree of the Knowledge of Good and Evil that Adam and Eve were forbidden to eat from in the book of Genesis? They were told that in the day they ate of it, they would surely die. The question behind the question was: Does God really love you, and if He does, then why is He withholding information from you?

It's a familiar question. Each of us wrestle with it on a constant basis. Why isn't God telling us what to do about our situation? He sees what's going on, yet He seems to remain silent. With all of the unrest in the world and the sad state of affairs we are in on this planet, there seems to be a coldness in the air that chills our very souls. What's missing? Could it be something as simple as this thing called love?

The Scriptures declare that God so loved the world that He gave His only begotten Son, that whosoever believes in Him shall not perish but have everlasting life (John 3:16). It couldn't have been easy for God to watch His created beings turn away from Him, instead of experiencing divine fellowship in a oneness that to this day cannot be accurately described in any human vernacular.

What I do know for sure is that when I operate from a place of love, it takes away my fear. Perfect love casts out fear, and fear has torment. How do we know if we're operating in love? We know when it's no longer about us and our feelings. When we press on through the awkwardness of being frightened and doing it anyway. When the fear of looking foolish and feeling "less than" has gone away. Love is the reason we obey when we see others the way our heavenly Father sees them.

In the airline industry, passengers are referred to as "souls on board" after a plane crash. I believe that's how we should see others all the time—as souls. We need to see people through the Father's eyes. The point that we begin giving of ourselves for the greater good instead of looking for instant gratification—that is the very moment when we can breathe a sigh of relief and get on with the business at hand of living life to the fullest. We are then able to enjoy the cohesiveness that comes with yielding, which in turn allows for someone else to flourish in their gift. How about that? It isn't all about me after all! Go figure. No wonder we are so stressed, anxious, and confused. That's what happens when we try to do everything ourselves and we refuse to relinquish control to someone else who is quite capable of getting the job done. It might not be to our specifications, but by not operating from a pure place of love, with no strings attached and with no ulterior motives, we lose the bond of humanity. We lose the fluidity that allows for a smooth transition from being egotistical to becoming compassionate, and beyond that, perhaps even empathetic. It becomes almost animalistic in our endeavor to scratch, kick, and fight our way to the top. The *top*? The *top* of what?

There's an old saying that "it's lonely at the top." The air is even thinner up there. It's harder to breathe, so you'll need supplemental oxygen to survive. The announcement on a plane during the safety briefing says to pull the mask over your face first and secure the straps. Even though oxygen *is* flowing, the mask may *not* appear to inflate. If there's someone needing assistance, you must put your own mask on first and then offer assistance. This is not a selfish act; in fact, it's an act of compassion. It's an act of love. You have got to take care of yourself before you can help anyone else. In other words, if I'm unconscious, how can I then help you? Try briefing a mother of an infant traveling with a lap child or child in arms, and tell her that she should place her own oxygen mask on first before helping her precious baby! At first it sounds cruel and inhumane—until she's able to take a moment and think about it. There are only seconds in an emergency to get air for yourself. The same applies to the flight attendants who are required to get on their own oxygen masks before trying to assist others, because they are the ones who are trained in an emergency to carry out a safe and timely evacuation in case one is needed on the ground.

And just how does this relate to love being the motivator to obey? Well, if we are not secure enough within ourselves to love ourselves and others, or to be at peace in order to follow directions even when it doesn't make sense at the time, then we won't be able to recognize that to obey is not a step down; it is indeed a giant leap of faith toward believing in a force that is far greater than anything we can comprehend as mere human beings. That force is *love*. Love trumps all!

First Corinthians 13 4 tells us what love is and what it is not. It's patient and kind; it doesn't boast; it's not proud or arrogant; it does not dishonor others; it is not self-seeking or easily angered; it keeps no record of wrongs. Love does not delight in evil, but it rejoices in the truth, and it always protects, trusts, hopes, and perseveres. Love never fails. Wow—just imagine living in a world motivated by love! It's not a fuzzy feeling, but rather, it's a conscious decision not to hate. It's God's plan for us, and it's who He is!

*Chapter 5*

# The Proof Is
# in the "Putting"

When putting love to the test, we find out what our true motivation is. As I began to challenge myself to put my total trust in God to lead and guide me in practical ways—and not just give Him lip service—it was clear to me that this was not going to be easy. I would have to face myself in order to see myself through His eyes, and I wasn't too sure I was up for the task. But if not now, when? Even though we understand that when we know the truth, the truth will make us free, we can't always handle the truth, as one very famous actor—Jack Nicholson—cried out in a popular scene from *A Few Good Men*. And when I say *can't*, I mean that we are not willing to accept it because it can be very uncomfortable. You would be surprised at the people who would just rather not know.

And I must say this: We all have a choice to accept it or ignore it. It's been said that the longest run we will ever have is the one to try to get away from ourselves. The whole running-in-circles lifestyle ended for me the moment I began to tune in to my inner man, and the Holy Spirit's promptings. That was the first time I was truly aware that it would require *courage to obey* what I believed. What exactly was it that I believed? That I could trust in the relationship into which I had invested so much quality time: the one between me and God the Father through His Holy Spirit.

Some might ask whether such a thing is even possible? Can a human being commune directly with a holy God? Should I ignore all the voices telling me that I can't prove it, and so no one would believe it was possible? I remembered I didn't have to prove anything to anybody. There's already a book—the Bible—that has recorded a host of believers' accounts! Everything within me was telling me that it was too hard to let go of the ideas that had governed my actions my whole life and jump out into an area with which I was unfamiliar. It was time to put up or shut up! I started praying and paying close attention to signs and little things that would come to mind. I no longer wanted to focus on the familiar and run the risk of missing out on divine direction. Not anymore. I decided that the proof was in the "putting." It was time to start putting into action what I taught, preached, and even counseled others to do.

When I returned to work after my leave, one day while on a break in between flights I walked into a restaurant to get something to eat when I wasn't even hungry. I went into the restaurant nonetheless, and I thought, "This is strange." I was seated and ordered lunch and noticed a woman sitting across from me engaged in a deep conversation. She seemed to be very emotional. As I turned to mind my own business, I couldn't help but overhear her conversation. She was discussing how her father was ill and she was being faced with having to make some difficult choices with regard to his health and personal affairs.

We both looked up at the same time and made eye contact, so I smiled. I knew in an instant why I was in that restaurant at that particular table and at that particular time. It was to talk to her. I didn't know how or what I was to say or even how I was supposed to approach her. But by now I had become familiar with the nudging of the Holy Spirit, because I had experienced it several times before.

Soon she hung up her phone. She looked up at me again and smiled. Her expression conveyed the sentiment: *I'm sorry I was talking so loud, and I hope I didn't disturb you.* I told her I had heard part of her conversation and asked if she would mind if I came and sat with her because I felt as if God wanted me to share some words with her. Awkward, yes, but courage trumps awkward every time. The proof was in her response. I had to put into action the thing that I felt "led" to do, because I understood that faith without works is dead. I simply had to trust my instincts and risk looking foolish. The ego is something else!

She seemed a bit surprised, but she welcomed me and pulled up a chair so that I could join her. What followed was nothing short of a miracle to me. A "chance encounter" would lead to an encounter with God's love pouring out of me to a soul who was desperately in need. I began telling her how I was in a similar situation with my mom and how I could relate to her pain. I shared how I sensed God's love for her, and I assured her that she was not alone.

As I continued to share what was on my heart, she reached out her hands to hold mine, and I watched her eyes fill with tears as she listened attentively, soaking up every word while gazing into my eyes. I felt her energy go from stressed to relaxed, and we were both aware that another force had just taken over, almost like air was seeping slowly from a balloon that had a pin-sized hole in it.

The waitress came with my food and noticed what was happening, and we both looked up at her and nodded to let her know that everything was alright. When I finished speaking, she began to cry and thank me for encouraging her. We hugged, and I assured her that it was God who had spoken through me and added that she must be a very important person to Him that He would have me come into a restaurant, order food even though I wasn't even hungry, and overhear her conversation just to tell her how much she was loved and not alone.

I went back to my table and was so glad I'd had the *courage to obey*. It took courage for me to step outside of my comfort zone and look past my own insecurities to see another human being in pain and then offer to get involved and not think twice about it. You would have to know me to understand how much of a loner I am. I am not typically a people person. I love people, but I am more comfortable keeping to myself. So, when I say I went out of my comfort zone in that experience, I've said a mouthful!

This world can sometimes be a cold place. As a result, we can become so caught up in our own lives until oftentimes we look right through another individual, not even seeing or hearing their cries for help. God's love is the one thing that can bring a sense of hope and warmth if we would only step away from our own selfishness and step away from the mentality that says it's all about me. Just one soul at a time is all it takes, but we must be willing to set our pride aside and be aware of our surroundings.

Our focus needs to be on God and His original plan for creating us. If you don't believe me, try putting yourself in someone else's shoes for a change and just watch how both your world and theirs can brighten up. It takes some effort to tune in to what the Holy Spirit is trying to show us on a moment-by-moment basis. There are opportunities all around us. We simply fail to see them because we become so engrossed in our own issues.

Just imagine what a world this could be if we all began to care again. In order for us to care for other people, we should get back to the basics. I can only share my experience and tell you how I have been able to accomplish this amazing feat in my own life. Since by the "foolishness of preaching" (see 1 Corinthians 1:21) I heard the gospel, or the good news, that God sent His Son, Jesus, to die upon the cross in my place and pay the penalty so that all who choose to believe in this unbelievable act of love could be saved from eternal separation from our heavenly Father and our Creator, I chose to accept it as truth. I confessed that I was a sinner, having been born through Adam and thus having the Adamic nature and being guilty when I was born into sin ("in sin did my mother conceive me" doesn't mean she wasn't married; it means that she, too, was a sinner when she was born, and so forth and so on). I asked Jesus to be my Lord and Savior, and by faith I now walk in newness of life through the guidance of the Holy Spirit.

I put it in those terms to explain or give more meaning to how I was able to make this transformation from self-indulgence to being aware of God and focused on His will and way. I was introduced to the fact that God cares, and not only that but that He cared for me. When we ask someone how they are and then actually listen for their response, it's amazing how it only takes a few moments to change someone's day for the better—by taking the time to care. The word *care* is powerful! One definition says that it is the provision of what is necessary for the health, welfare, maintenance, and protection of someone or something. Another one puts it this way: Serious attention or consideration is applied to doing something correctly or to avoid damage or risk.

Wow! Do you know what that says to me? It says that by simply caring about how another person's day is going or that they may be hurting or that they are even having a wonderful experience or have something to share, it can possibly enhance your life or reroute your way of thinking and inspire you!

I have hundreds of stories just like the one I shared earlier, where one thing led to another. They were seemingly random situations—but not so random after all, almost as if they were orchestrated by a mastermind who had everything already figured out. One who sits up high and looks down low. One who sees all and knows all. The omnipresent, omniscient One. God almighty! Yes, I call Him "God," and if you're offended, then that's your right to be. We all have choices and I respect everyone's right to believe in God or not. But this is my faith experience, and I choose to share it with those who are interested. He has proven Himself to me time and time again.

I don't need to prove anything to anyone, because truth be told I can't prove it—not tangibly anyway. God is Spirit, and those who worship Him must worship Him in spirit and in truth (John 4:24). The important thing is that I choose to believe in Him by faith in His Word, and you can, too, or not. For God so loved the world that He gave His only begotten Son so that whosoever believes in Him should not perish but have everlasting life (John 3:16).

Whether you're a Christian or not, acts of kindness go a mighty long way. Pay it forward whenever you can. All parties involved reap the benefits. It's true—we do reap what we sow, the good as well as the bad. We often only hear that quoted in a negative, threatening way, as if to say, "Watch out, God's gonna getcha!" There certainly are consequences to sin (i.e., missing the mark); as Romans 6:23 tells us, "For the wages of sin is death, but the gift of God is eternal life through Christ Jesus". Sin is rebellion against something we know to be true. When we are separated from the truth, we wander around stumbling in error. But we must remind ourselves that there are rewards to making the mark. Put God first and seek His Kingdom, and all these things will be added unto you, according to Matthew 6:33. What things? The things that you need in order to live.

*Chapter 6*

# What's My Motivation?

Obedience without the right motivation is futile. It's simply empty compliance. You'll more than likely regret choosing to obey at some point, once you're not *feeling it anymore*. This false humility doesn't require any courage, and it doesn't last for very long. Also, there's no peace that accompanies this type of robotic action.

Hebrews 11:25 tells us that Moses chose to suffer or be mistreated with the children of God rather than to enjoy the pleasures of sin for a season. Love was behind it all. He had a love for God and for his native people. That *makes all the difference* in not quitting when it doesn't feel good to obey your inner convictions. He might not have even been aware of why he was drawn to the Hebrew people at first, but he knew their God. God's love for him and his love for God was worth it all! Hebrews 11:25 tells us that he chose to look past the initial suffering, and instead he looked toward the big picture. For we know that the sufferings of this present time are not worthy to be revealed to the glory that shall be revealed in us.

We cannot operate from that place if we're always looking for instant gratification. It cannot be born out of a stony heart, but a pliable one, one softened by a love so powerful that it gave Jesus the strength to suffer, shed His innocent blood, and die so that those who believe in Him, repent of their sin, and ask Him to come into their hearts might have eternal life with Him. Until we can grasp the passion of the cross, we won't be able to obey without resentment and rebellion. I don't believe we are capable, with our finite understanding and without the Holy Spirit's help.

When we see ourselves as stuck or forced to obey, that is when we tend to feel helpless and hopeless. It can seem like we have lost power or control. That must be how Eve felt in the Garden when she was faced with the possibility that the God she'd come to know and love didn't *really* love her, as was suggested by the serpent, or He wouldn't have held back this *one* tree from her. She no longer wanted to obey, because the love that she had been so secure in was now being challenged. Perfect love cast out fear, but now through a seed of doubt that had so subtly been planted by the serpent, suddenly fear crept in. Tormented by a suggestion that she no longer possessed what she thought she had, she was left feeling like she was missing out on something.

Have you ever noticed that we start to panic when we think we're not included? Have you ever found out about a party or a gathering that your friends were invited to, yet you knew nothing about? Immediately something dark and negative wells up inside! We start to question—hopefully inwardly— *Why didn't I know about this? Why wasn't I invited?* Just check social media and look at all the "comments" from *random* people you didn't even know liked you, or better yet, who even *knew* you! I'm not even on social media like that, but I have seen it whenever I am. It can be a form of rejection, and rejection is said to be extremely devastating to the human psyche.

Eve suddenly lost her motivation. She was no longer content. Now there was this nagging question as to why "He" would keep this one thing from her. There used to be a respect that she felt toward God. Notice how suddenly the reverence was no longer there. A sense of familiarity had begun to set in.

I don't know about you, but I certainly have felt this way at times when I started listening to the voice of doubt, and when I second-guess what I knew to be true. The thing that I was once so confident in now would suddenly seem to be a mistake! What about all that she *did* have access to? It no longer satisfied. It was no longer enough. The same thing happens to us when we think we have to know everything. There's no need for trust if we already know it all. Let's commit to trusting the One who *does* know it all, God, the Supreme Being. There is so much peace that accompanies cooperating with the instructions of the One who has a proven track record.

There's an old song that says, "Oh, what peace we often forfeit, oh, what needless pain we bear, all because we do not carry, everything to God in prayer." When we're no longer motivated, it kills our drive and it becomes a struggle for us to continue without some more information. Our whole attitude changes—as did Eve's. Be careful who or what you let convince you that you are suddenly no longer content. Godliness with contentment is great gain.

Guard your heart, as King Solomon admonished us to do in Proverbs 4:23.

I know in my own life that just when I finally get my momentum and my faith is built up after reading and hearing the Word of God, and I'm trusting God with my whole heart, the tiniest, most negative, unproductive thought can creep in and knock the wind right out of me. I have to stop, get my bearings, collect myself, and ask myself what the hell just happened. My point is that I don't even talk like that, but it's organic to phrase it that way. When you start off on the right track but after a while look around, only to find yourself in a strange place, simply going through the motions, then it might be a good time to ask yourself just what *is* your motivation.

*Chapter 7*

# The Final Word

*L*ove is the final word. I know this sounds "cheesy." How predictable, you say. Love, love, love. What's love got to do with it? Well, I'm glad you asked. It's got *everything* to do with it! Without it, we would not exist. God's love imagined us and spoke us into existence. God *is* love, and we are made in His image. The whole point of this book is to steer us back toward love.

We often ask what can be done about the condition in which we now find this world. What we can do as individuals is get back to loving one person at a time. Get back to God. If you don't believe in Him, then this message may not be for you. It's a matter of choice. I choose to believe in a God that I can't even tangibly prove to you exists. I choose to run the risk of looking like a complete fool in the face of those around me by believing in a God I am not humanly able to explain. Love is not a feeling but an act or an action. It's not that I'm being passive or burying my head in the sand or hoping for the good ol' bye-and-bye. I simply refuse to wrestle with trying to force someone to give me answers to questions that at the end of the day won't even matter. Just ask Job about his experience when he dared to ask God to answer him.

First Corinthians 13:12 reminds us that we see through a glass darkly, but then we will see face-to-face. In other words, we don't get to know everything! I had the privilege to spend some precious time with my oldest sister as she was preparing to leave this world. I was able to listen closely to what was important and what was not even worth fretting over. I have been around a few people who were at the end of this life as we know it, and the same message was expressed to me. Can we please not wait until the end to learn this great lesson?

Love is what is important above all else. Love is the common thread that ties us all together. *L O V E* to me is letting our vibe explode in such a way that everyone around us is encouraged to take another step and try again—because at the end of the day, we all need one another.

To order additional copies of

# *Courage To Obey*

please visit www.amazon.com

Also visit the author's website

Oneofakindchristiancounseling.com

www.ingramcontent.com/pod-product-compliance
Lightning Source LLC
Chambersburg PA
CBHW071435040426
42445CB00012BA/1369